Title: "James Baldwin: A Journey of Truth and Forgiveness"
ISBN: 978-1-966163-25-1
Author: Norma McLauchlin
Illustrated by: Jasmine Price
Chosen Pen Publishing, LLC

James Baldwin
A Journey of Truth and Forgiveness

James Baldwin was a powerful writer and activist who spoke out against injustice. His story is not just about his fight for equality but also about the importance of forgiveness in understanding one another.

James Baldwin was born on August 2, 1924, in New York City. He grew up in a large family and faced many challenges, including poverty and discrimination.

From a young age, James loved to read and write. He found joy in expressing his thoughts and feelings through words, which would become his lifelong passion.

Baldwin used his writing to explore the complexities of race, identity, and love. His words resonated with many and shed light on the struggles of being Black in America.

- GO TELL IT ON THE MOUNTAIN
- ANOTHER COUNTRY — JAMES BALDWIN
- IF BEALE STREET COULD TALK — JAMES BALDWIN
- ANOTHER COUNTRY
- TELL ME HOW LONG THE TRAIN BEEN GONE
- IF BEALE STREET COULD TALK — JAMES BALDWIN
- NOTES of a NATIVE SON — JAMES BALDWIN
- COLLECTED ESSAYS — JAMES BALDWIN
- ESSAYS — JAMES BALDWIN

James Baldwin became a leading voice in the civil rights movement. He traveled around the country, speaking about the importance of justice and equality for all people.

Throughout his life, Baldwin understood that anger and hatred could divide people. He believed that forgiveness was essential for healing and understanding across communities.

12

Baldwin wrote powerful essays, such as 'Notes of a Native Son,' where he explored his experiences with racism and the need for empathy and forgiveness.

James Baldwin believed that through open dialogue and forgiveness, people could bridge divides and work together to create a more just society.

16

James Baldwin's legacy as a writer and activist continues to inspire people today. He showed us that truth-telling and forgiveness are powerful tools for change.

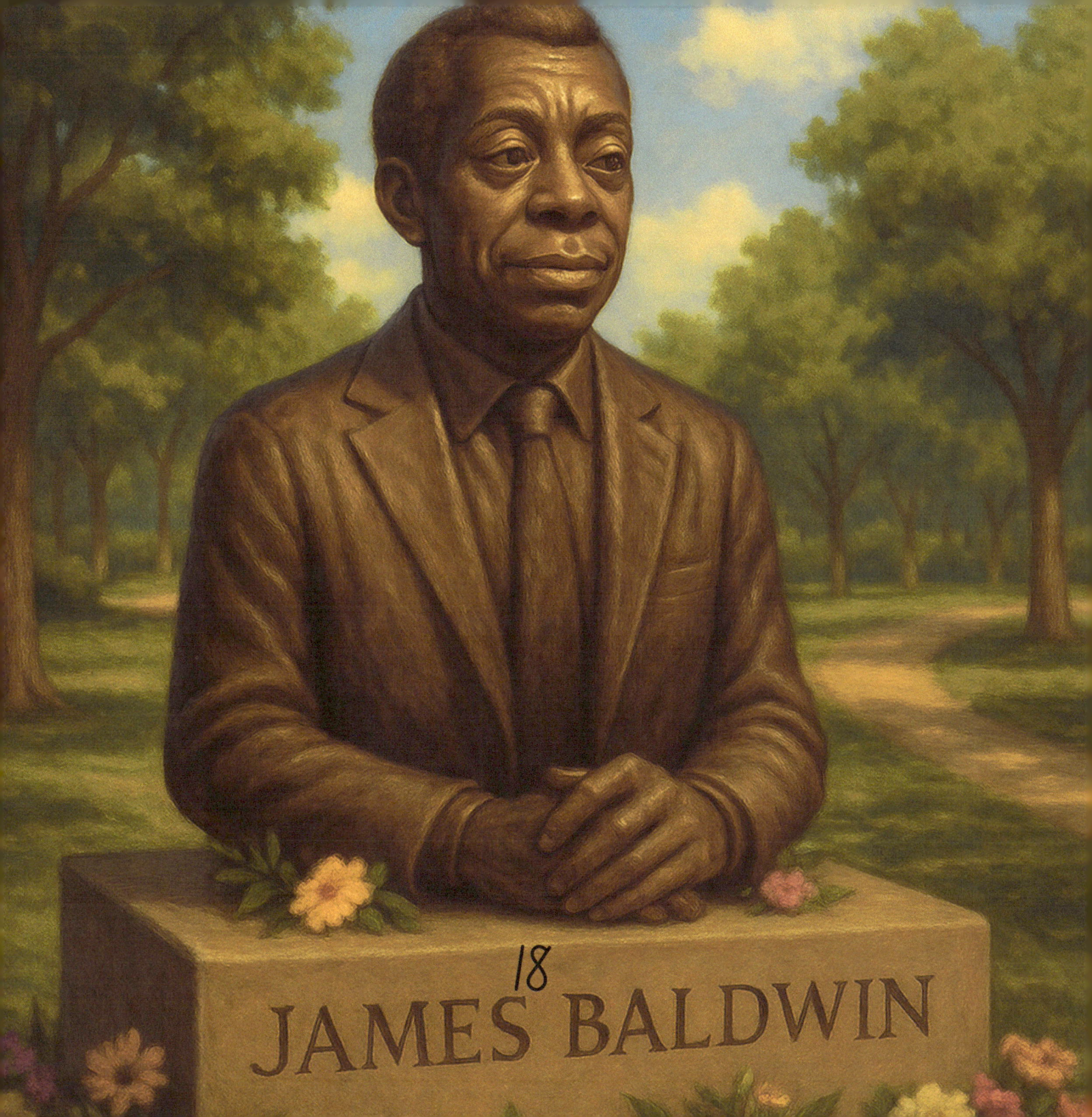

Today, James Baldwin inspires writers, activists, and thinkers to speak their truth and embrace forgiveness in their own lives.

Baldwin once said, 'Not everything that is faced can be changed, but nothing can be changed until it is faced.' Let's remember his words and face the truth together.

Just like Baldwin, we can all make a difference. Whether it's standing up for a friend or learning about our history, we can create positive change together.

24

Baldwin knew that working together was essential for change. Let's build a community of kindness and forgiveness.

Acts of kindness and forgiveness can change lives. Let's remember James Baldwin's example and treat everyone with respect and compassion.

28

James Baldwin dreamed of a world where everyone was treated equally. Let's keep that dream alive by working together and forgiving one another.

Now it's your turn! How will you make a difference? Think about what you can do to help others and stand up for what is right.

32

James Baldwin showed us that with courage, determination, and compassion, we can change the world. Forgiveness is a key part of that change.

34

Let's celebrate hope, kindness, and justice for everyone. Together, we can build a world where all are treated equally.

James Baldwin's life was a journey of truth and forgiveness. He taught us that even in the face of hardship, we can choose to forgive and help others.

Additional titles in this series:

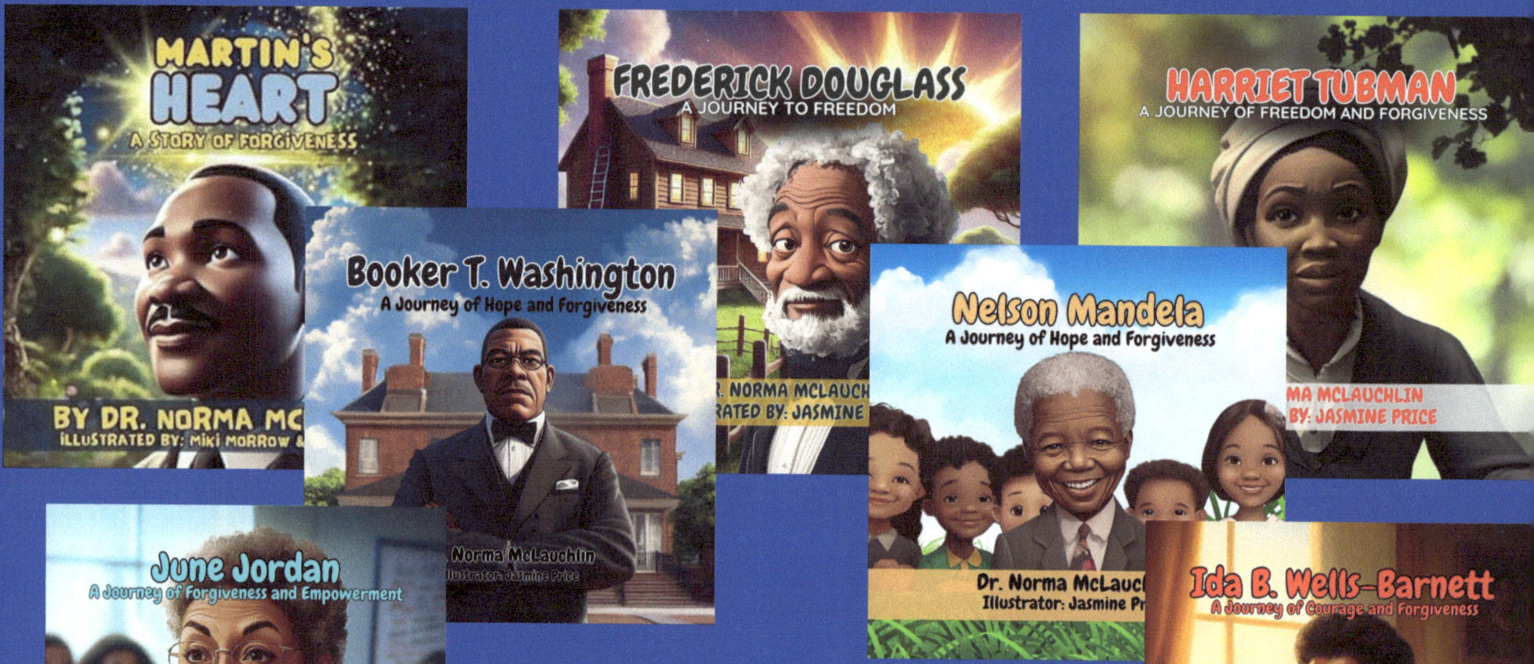

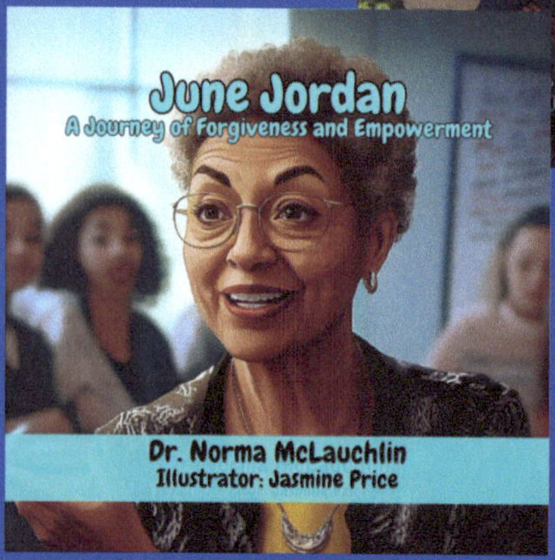

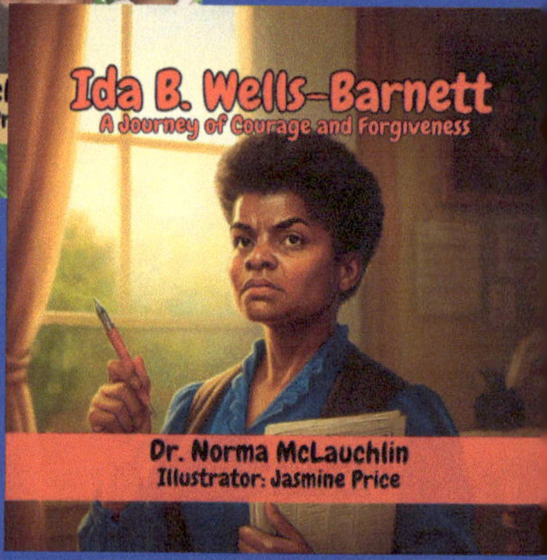

Look out for more exciting titles!

www.ingramcontent.com/pod-product-compliance
Lightning Source LLC
Chambersburg PA
CBHW042004150426
43194CB00002B/120